STILL LIFE
WITH
JUDAS
&
LIGHTNING

POEMS

STILL LIFE
WITH
JUDAS
&
LIGHTNING

POEMS

Dawn Diez Willis

Airlie Press is supported by book sales and subscription orders,
by contributions to the press from its supporters,
and by the work donated by all the poet-editors of the press.

Major funding has been provided by:

Terry Brix
Jim & Tara & Lucas Savage
Mr. & Mrs. W. W. Shaner
Julia Wills

Cover art: Klaus Whitley
Author photo: Cassandra Rae
Design: Cheryl McLean
Paul Celan epigraph appears by permission of Persea Books.

Airlie Press
PO Box 434
Monmouth, OR 97361
airliepress@yahoo.com
www.airliepress.org

ISBN 978-0-9821066-8-6
Library of Congress Control Number: 2013939470

Printed by Thomson-Shore on 30% postconsumer recycled paper
Processed chlorine-free

Printed in the United States of America

for Kevin, Djuna, and Sinjin

The stone.
The stone in the air, which I followed.
Your eye, as blind as the stone.

We were
hands,
we baled the darkness empty, we found
the word that ascended summer:
flower.

from "Flower" by Paul Celan
translation by Michael Hamburger

Contents

☽

〜

Young Couple Marries in July

On their wedding day: white pellet rain of rice and clear light.
Her cheeks fruited, his smile guileless as bread.
Some life before them the celebrants could taste:
lavender and plum and a third element unnamed.

The community bore gifts in colored bowls and gleaming foil.
The elders fanned flies.
The children gamboled, sugar-fed,

and threw their shoes into the elm-shade and ran
away with shrieks of celebration.

Bride and groom waltzed on a floor laid across summer grass.
Between them, beneath white froth,
beneath pretty girl-fat and viscera,
a spoonful of baby sat at the center.

It was all for her: rice and light, flower and foil,
flies and shrieks and limitless wonder across the grass.

Runaway Slave Resting in the Brush at Dawn

There is an unknowable life called *out there, beyond,*
and a knowable life called *abomination.*
There is an unknowable life: *children in lamplight*
playing jacks, coffee after the long day, wages and privacy's clean shadows.
There is a knowable life: *congealed scrap in the chest,*
nausea's acrid flowers, tasks with tails off the end of the earth.
There is a knowable life to be had every day,
and an unknowable life that might not be had no matter the act.
There is the fat sun that rises on both.
And here it is, casting its coins of shadow over your face.

Collection

Through the penitentiary gate, he is released.
He can see his sister come to collect him,
a woman walking across a hot black sea
made miraculous by the wonder of his freedom.

She wears the broken cheekbones of their childhood,
her smile a scattering of gulls.

He walks to her car slowly with his
plastic bag of nothing, released
into this current, the one he dreamed a decade,
each waiting day a small chamber in a nautilus shell.
The air touches every part of him.
The sun knows him now but could not in that place.

In her Ford Fiesta, his sister lights his cigarette from hers,
and they breathe the gray privacy of smoke,
hold the silence between them, gathering its shapely seconds.

They reach his mother's rented house: cracked walk
dividing the sand-colored lawn in two, balloons
tied on bright ribbons to each railing, to the eaves of the roof,
to the handlebars of his nephews' motocross bikes.
They are everywhere like jellyfish, trembling and harmless.

Each living member of his family holds one bobbing on a length
of gift-wrap ribbon: cousins, nephews and nieces, aunts and uncles,
his mother, and his daughter, who is thirteen and has a lock
of hair glistening and sprayed into a tendril on her forehead.

His mother begins to run on her heavy legs.
Shy of him, his daughter watches the white balloons tug in the light.
He stays in the car. Its closed windows and cell of heat.

Sun glitters off of every surface containing him.
We'll go to the ocean tomorrow, his sister is saying,
doors unlocking with sharp snaps.
You can collect shells again when you have somewhere to put them.

Two View Drive-In, Mission Beach

A berry field now paved over in asphalt
with poles at intervals emitting voices
and a story enormous above
the many vehicles parked in rows—
the field could almost sigh beneath them.
It had its own story once: bramble and foot-traffic
and pails stained in bright juice.
Now, more than one girl a night looks above her boy's
dark head to the blacktop sky and the moon careless
as a bared thigh above them all.
The magic boxes fastened to the windows
crackle and rasp sentences from those new futures,
stories seeking root above the field.

Lacy Learning Eve

Home from church, she thinks of what she's heard:
a woman not yet occurred, sealed inside,
a *C* of bone waiting to be plucked out
by the voice of the tide.

Could a woman be a rib? She could, they'd said,
the man's body holding her in place
like one string of a violin.

Near Eve's ear, Adam's liver
sang its pond of songs,
let the future's music muffle through.

Lacy puts her pillow lightly over her face.
Her closed eyelids sparkle with colored gnats,
a scattering of notes.

No father sang the song of her name or ever
plucked her up from the day's design.
She is only her mother's child, but she is also
the little morsel waiting to be called out
from an unlit, unchosen place

where she lives as if in a cistern of sound,
where she is fastened like the nameless leaf of a tree.

Trapeze in Autumn

The light through the small, high window
touches his face, retreats, then touches again,
warm and yellow and full of motes.
The trapeze Grandpa hung in the barn
swings the boy gleefully, his body
rushing through the hot air
face-first, then backward
like an indecisive bird.
Fearful joy bursts up through his torso
and with his whole mouth he tastes fast air,
his smile showing teeth of milk and vegetables
and running through summer grass.

Swinging too high, he never sees the pipe,
flight blinding him to the space where it waits.
Big, new teeth, the ones that separate
the boys from the babies,
smash from their gums and burst
into a thick mouthful of blood.
The trapeze pulls him backward
through the strange, hot space of the barn.
Of course he wants to call for his mother,
but she is gone.

In bed that night, the pink gap
aches like a fresh grief.
He'd spit blood and saliva and calcium chips
into the sink, his aunt holding his head,
making woman sounds, pressing a warm
washcloth of salt water into the bloodied gap.
In bed, he pokes his tongue carefully
through the raw, torn space.
The dark moves in close
and crickets flip fast pebbles

of sound against the window glass.
Eyeing the waving door,
he moves his thumb toward his mouth.
It tastes of soap.
No stars nick the window;
he can't make a wish.
His mother calls and calls somewhere
with a mouthful of death.
He could count the steps to her
and walk them.

Socorra at the Pond

Socorra comes to wade and listen hard,
ankles parting drifts of foam.
Her whole skin remembers floating
with her sister in the pond
behind their grandmother's house,
the taste of green water
and the walk home together,
towel-draped and famished.

A damselfly steps across
the surface, born to do so.
If she could, Socorra would too,
sure that would be the height
required to hear, to know what
her sister wants to say in that light,
that wind, that rustle of unspeaking beings.

The steps of the damselfly's needle legs
form radiating circles on the water
filigreed in scum, verdigris, and tiny eggs.

This is where her sister's voice lives now,
rustle and hum, cicada tide at twilight,
circles that move out toward life.

Second Week in Foster Care

Days are quiet. Nights too.
Still, they have a mother somewhere,
riven and ravaged, lost to them.
Both want her back, want to sit on her lap,
grasp at the gray smoke forced through her lips,
smell the ammonia salt of her skin.
They want their own mother,
blood-bonded and love-hobbled,
the mother of fault and foil and belt,
the woman with the story of their birth
and some afternoons together in ease.
She is theirs and they are hers even
as they sleep in their new mother's home.
One child's mouth is stoppered in a pink pacifier.
Another tugs his ear reflexively in dreams.
They do not yet want the woman who watches
over sleep, changes wet sheets, or folds tired clothes,
that almost-mother who took the call in the dark
to receive them, each barefoot,
each carrying a paper bag and a seamed, speechless animal.

Lost Daughter & Palm Trees

Fronds of palm trees cut the sky with silhouettes,
jagged stencils staining the twilight.
Her small boy organizes plastic men,
her middle daughter lies on her bed
among the leaves of candy wrappers.
Someone is missing. They keep hoping she'll return.

Folding T-shirts and underpants, the woman
remembers the soft yipping of the neighbor's dogs,
milk bottles chiming their daily music,
her father's leafy newspaper
sighing in the twilight.
How quiet was her childhood:
walking in the weeds, picking
strawberries for supper.
Outside each night, they saw the edge of a field and sky.

Palm trees cut open the purpling sky with fronds.
The night is cool and still, the warm smoke
from her cigarette filling her chest
with some icy singing caught there.
She'll call again tomorrow
for her missing girl, will play the cassette
of her daughter's loved music on the way to work.

Smashing the white butt, she realizes
how she hates those palm trees,
their hissing and insistence,
their pointed shapes that will not be changed.

Surviving the Trail

As she crossed the Great Salt Lake Desert
on foot behind the wagons,
she'd carried her one child in her arms,
glad to have only one, and thought her arms
would drop him, but found she could do
what she didn't think she could.
He was a heavy child even without food for days
but she carried him, walking toward the edge
of the white-hot earth, not getting any closer.

At night, at the end of those months, when
they'd survived as some others had not,
and ate every night, and even
owned a few things again, she used to kneel
to watch the boy she'd carried under
the white eye of unblinking sun.
He'd slept in cool sheets
held by something beyond her.

She tries to pray, tries to find the whisper of some
merciful eternity in her belly or bone.
Did something see it all?
Did something have a hand in what occurred?
Six months into safety, he died of cholera.
Kingdom. Kingdom.
Her nails press their wagon spokes into her palms.

Billy on the Train

At every stop, Billy jumps down and runs
to the same car. Inside, he touches a long box.

His hands rest flat against it.
The train's whistling makes people

restless and melancholy for miles
as the train moves again, not in the imperceptible

way of the earth, but lurching and rocking
its way toward speed, toward destination.

The train moves and he finds the loss
behind the skin has reasons.

The moon outlives us. This is one.
At every stop the boy checks his cargo:

You alright, Mom?
His lips cold against the lid.

He can hear the train's life, see the passing miles.
The train travels so much faster than the earth

and the boy loves to go fast, the way
everything rushes hard to get behind you.

Fidela at the San Felipe de Neri Museum

Inside the museum: robes, christening gowns,
ledgers, a tarnished censer, ceiling beams
like whole trees felled and risen horizontal.
In the smaller back room, the walls are curved.
A box, draped in wrinkled fabric,
color of eggshells, color of a nimbus,
holds a life-sized marionette of Jesus.
His puppet knees seem broken, stained in the cracks,
thighs and shins separated. A note card clarifies:
Jesus' knees weren't broken during the crucifixion.
Leather straps allow his joints to bend.
When Lent comes, parishioners will haul him
onto their shoulders, carry him through the streets,
create a finale affixing him to the cross
at the altar by holes drilled into his limbs.

Fidela puts her paper cup of coffee to her lips,
looking down at him, wanting to peel him
from his straw bed, heft him to her shoulder
like an unwieldy baby, let his limbs clatter
on the sunlit cobbles of Albuquerque,
give freedom to what doesn't even live.
There is nothing she believes in
that will change anyone or free them.

Pneumonia & Smoke

The broken bird of belief calls
preacher, preacher, preacher
from the lawn of childhood.
Lynn thinks it accuses her as her thoughts do:
you made the baby sick with dark thinking.
Her husband, her mother-in-law agree,
and they pray together near the crib slats.
They weed their thoughts, believe.
Still, the baby girl wheezes, flutters fists.
Lynn stands, takes up the girl, runs to the car.
On the drive, examining her conscience,
she tries to remove each wrong thought,
but each returns, flies that will not be waved off.
Past the sliding hospital doors, she seeks
the stark declarations of prayer,
struggles to construct her thoughts like little
cathedrals of straw, and hands the baby
to the wordless, white-clad nurse.
To her left, she sees the smokers in their special room.
Their ashen cords reach up to touch
the hopeful ceiling tiles above their tired heads.
When she joins them, the smokers do not ask her
if she wants the baby to be sick.
They are more practical.
They believe in misfortune.

Adam's Third Son

One son killed the other, everyone knew,
but there was one more after,
born in the shadow of grieving.
The third boy had waited tucked behind his father's scapula.
He had been a gleam across the grain and copper,
the golden oil illuminated in the glass.

He arrived at the sad hearth and cried his needs
and awakened the family to the world that remains
when the murdered and murderer have gone
and we must eye each other carefully
and keep tending to the sheep and the baby.

Etchings

A needle pushes the curls
of bitumen: alphabet of trees,
planets of three nectarines,
ocean of a shallow bowl, a woman's
starfish hand paused in organizing.

Like a curette, the tools remove what
ruins the print, what prevents.

Hana Is *Flower*

Two languages twine like reluctant fingers.
Ink speckles his desk, and papers
tessellate across its surface.
In his University office, Hitoshi looks
out his open window, the air
sweetened by white blossoms in each tree.

In one hour, he will lie on the sidewalk outside the building.
A man is waiting to teach him *sharp*,
to teach him *last* in some language he can't yet know.

But for now, the scholar daydreams,
turning in his chair like a cradle,
almost reaching toward the four
trees he can see past the glass,
thinking *ki* means *tree*, thinking
tree means *ki*.

The Artists' Angels

Petrus Christus and Hans Memling give to Mary—
adored vessel—a tiara of auric rods
poking up through her pensive young scalp
like a cosmic migraine of blessedness.

Domenico Veneziano makes shadows like unlit fish,
magic men with limpid faces and drapes,
and little caps of wonderment red-edged.
Or the seraph sending down its strings with their
five-pointed sources of crimson insistence.

Van Eyck and Bernini embody the unseen forces
as an array of slender yellow rods,
knitting needles of the cosmos come to pierce
the seeker with ecstasy and dread.

Or think of del Cossa's St. Lucy, holding
the lorgnette of her own two eyes
with such sly, surprised acceptance.

Enshrined Outlaw as Seven Relics

His name rings like a spur,
like a loose bit in the mouth
of a riderless horse, or the star
precarious on its rusty pin.

He kept a woman waiting
in a lonely house on a wide
and wind-blown piece of land,
and she could hear the jangle in his speech:
tinsel and jasper and a clutch of jonquils
all her days.

Supper sent up steam
like surrendered hands
while Jesse said *grace*,
and Pinkertons flew through the county
like skinny, brainless devils.
They'd never make it.

O, the cold trains,
cold banks, with the *o*
of a gun in a stunned face,
mortality's bright blue bolts
piercing frozen passengers
whispering prayers for him
and his boys to turn
backs to the brain-spilling,
dust-catching air, to swirl
like some crazy dervishes,
and vanish.

❦

Zee could hear it like a cough,
faint punctuation in the parlor.
Even as Jesse became a fine
daddy with a clean moustache
and a starched shirt, she could smell it:
jonquils, rot, and their babies rib by rib.

❦

Jesse could feel it wanting to be near him,
wanting a souvenir of skin, wanting
to make him well like a doctor
with a jar of leeches, like a sword impaling
his days, or like the bright,
caustic tonics ringing in the pockets
of the black-eyed Man Himself.

❦

He couldn't shake the dream:
a surgeon wiping and wiping
a rusty blade across an apron,
Jesse's suit coat darkening.

Hagar & the Blue Jay at the Buena Vista Apartments

The baby first comes to her
as a dream of a blue jay streaming light.
It is a warning about blessing and nature.

Two bodies twine like purple clematis
and the bargain grows. The couple settles,
agrees without smiles, feels the linkage
of the soul and gristle.

Soon, the woman holds the newborn swaddled in cotton.
Everything is changed. There is no going back.
The jay on the yellowed apartment lawn
pecks the thoughtless insects
and eyes her somehow.

Though love is sometimes in her throat like a swallowed dime,
there is something she wants and cannot name.
She will always want it now.
Her glass ashtray fills with the gray powder
of trying to know what some other life could be
if she had not lain down
like a little corpse of joy in the birdsong.

Girl with Greenstick Fracture

Often she thinks of things twined in white:
lovers' teeth, peonies neat in clear glass,
wings that ceaselessly beat.

Sometimes her will is a sheer peignoir
slipped off at the feet, little white puddle of beauty.
She will retrieve it later, limping, touching a rib.

Sometimes the nearness of *something*
moves her eyelashes, caresses her cheek.
She believes it's for a reason but can't name it.

Still, it is not all purpled eye and cracked teeth,
knuckles unsheathed and time punched dumb.
It is also love-struck palms on sheets,

the limpid eye of light, sweet stir of gloss and pubis.
It is remorse, orange and florid as poppies.
Somewhere within: an oasis of light and the soul's seat.

Sometimes his hips are the flanks she is riding away.
Sometimes her voice emerges like smooth eggs
one at a time: colorless, frictionless, without flaw—

little rabbits of want from the depth of a black burrow.
It is not all electric cords, seepage in gauze, time stopped,
or the center of herself dissolved and leaking,

or reproachful nurses ministering when something breaks.
Sometimes crown to sole, every gingery morsel of her skin sings.
Sometimes just TV and laughter. Sometimes a kiss.

Sometimes, like a bird from a pocket, she appears:
a fragment reborn in his hot light,
warm feathers overlaying the bone and glass beneath.

Young Widow in the Field

Limping with loss, she walks through wheat
and a horizon of smoke and bleach.
Clean laundry weighs down the straw basket she carries,
her head full of yellow staples of what's true.
Whatever sustained her before
doesn't exist anymore, though the field is there
and makes her remember his body,
how his skin of grit and grasses
would mark her for days.

Knowing it is true won't dissolve
in the stirring of first coffee,
won't slip away in the topaz stream
of dish soap across her evening plate.
The animal in the wheat field can only wait
while the sun comes and goes.

Cold tea in a yellow cup on her nightstand.
How many weeks has it been there?
When she climbs too early into the white bed,
her body slips within the palea of wheat-colored sheets
and travels deep hours in the ground
to the time before she knew
and then to the morning, the pause
before the threshing of sulfur light.

When Lazarus Comes Back

Opening stiff eyelids, he sees the World again:
the walls too white, the air too close with decomposing flesh.

Coming to his senses, he reclaims the fine
light surging in his eyes, the dust, sand,

flakes of skin floating in his nostrils, the foul
stewed taste of his own tongue, the hiss of wind

moving in and out of stone, in and out of lung,
the texture of minerals through the wrapped

and rotting pads of his revived fingers.
Sitting up on the stone where he was placed

with hard grief and finality, Lazarus can see
light where the sealing stone used to be.

He can see a figure: barefoot, expressionless,
waiting for him as the flat shape of a man.

Sunlight pierces Lazarus as he steps toward the man,
and the crowd, waiting for a miracle, hates the sight

of Lazarus, hates the jerk of his walk, the dirty
bandages blowing, his dumb surprise at rejoining them.

Some scream, wail, cover their faces.
Some lose their ability to speak and stagger home.

Some throw sand until the air is alive with it.
And the figure holds out his hands to Lazarus.

And the figure walks across the sand to meet him
halfway. *Welcome* someone says into his bandaged ear

and the crowd gathers its fear
like a tool of the field and goes to work.

Friday Night Wake in June

Mother's body lies cooling, dusk
gilding her a little.
Brother and sister refuse
to hold hands like good orphans.

The girl has the open, silvery look of a fish.
She twitches in the patio pool of evening,
weaving between the stalks of neighbors' legs.

Somewhere now, the boy hides in a tree
in his good clothes, listening,
watching the sun sink to bed.

The girl shakes in her laced shoes.
The mosquitoes don't care a stitch
and fly through the bark smell of coffee.
Grains of sugar collect on the cloth.

Grief sounds all through the house.
It is the sound of people eating.
It is the sound of the sound behind words.

Bonnie in the Woods

Maybe it's the trees, silent and ready,
driving them to it with whispers
as Bonnie teeters on Clyde's narrow
shoulders like a child riding
her daddy to anywhere.
Her knees grip, hold her steady,
and she tilts her chin, lets the sky
try to eat her up with its greedy blue.

Something is pushing them forward.
Something hovers in the woods
along single, stretching roads
and it doesn't know a fugitive
from a decent, upstanding citizen,
will house them both in spruce,
kill either with cold given half a chance.

Something craves the span
of her ankles dangling there,
has an uncomfortable itch
to snap their bones
like the necks of warm birds.

Face to the sky, she can't be sure
that later bullets will pierce her
as if sewing her with sunlight,
those blurry yellow threads undone.
She can't be positive her Clyde
will burst with red patterns in the woods,
dance among the quivering trees
until the bullets are finished
and unstring him too.
There is a sick love in the bullets,
unearthly and long.

Clyde puts her down to the ground
and she lies with him on his offered jacket.
This moment is passing.
She kisses between his light-pierced eyes,
her romance man, her one true.
When their lips meet, time stops
in his hot, quiet tracks, still as a person
with hands in the air.

She can hear some narrator etching them
into the permanence of words.
She can hear the voice taking it down,
telling the rumors about love
and its rued perfumes.

Maybe it's the trees, silent and ready.
Or maybe the sun, teetering
in its own stillness as her body
floats up to meet Clyde's,
a cloud blown loose
from its bright blue backing.

The Rinsing Sink

She sweeps the snipped hair into a plastic dustpan.
Combs and brushes float in blue formaldehyde.
Wiping three pairs of scissors,
the electric razor with its sliding teeth,
the false leather of the swiveling seat,
the deep burn in her womb
feels like peroxide left too long on the scalp.
She imagines the scrapings
as a human pulp among
sticky plastic instruments
and will not have time today to imagine more.
Now nothing hovers at the rim of her days
and the bare basin of her body resonates.
She moves to rinse the clinging
hairs of strangers from her sink.
Soon she will greet the newcomer, settle her,
turn her to the oval mirror, change
the future with an instrument's sharpened edges.

Martha Observes Jesus Working

Between the dishes and the chicken roasting,
she watches the healings, those brilliant amputations,
those excisions of the spirit with parings and rinds invisible.
Each person comes to him, some tentative, some
desperate, each quivering with hope and wounding.
When it happens, the air wavers as if cooking-fire
smoke has risen up around them.
Sometimes she thinks she sees him reach in and pull out
the spine of suffering, translucent and tined,
held up to the light for inspection and admiration.
Deftly, each night, she guts a dinner fish, defeathers a hen,
watches through the door space.
Each seeker is a fish, a bird, that needs to be prepared.
After supper, she wipes the crumbs, rinses
the cups, sweeps the ash that is left,
throws scraps of bone, skin, and organ to the hungry dogs.

Linseed Oil

Green beans dangle on their window vines.
Petunias insist their indigo beauties.
Sometimes she paints them together.
Sometimes half-finished in her heart,
bean and petal spill out of the frame, unfinished.
She loves or not. She is loved or not.
The sunlight through the jar of linseed oil
is her epiphany, its prism of yellow attention.
The brushes prickling out of a water glass
are Bernini's little rods toward Teresa.

John Eight

The work of wanting doesn't wear away
but brightens a pearl into gleam
as she labors under the blanket,
morning easing its belly-colored rays into the room.
Her husband sleeps still.

Washrag of light on a lover's limbs—

She thinks of slipping out a window into the desert:
endless dunes, peeling sun,
her remains a painting of salt on the sand
for Bedouins to piss on as they pass.

Mysterious curve cleaving—

She thinks it has almost been worth
what is about to occur—
being dragged through the streets,
dropped at a man's feet.
Everyone who knows her and some who do not
will hold a stone.

Her skull, her bones might remain whole,
but her share of sin, its sheens, its curving arc,
will be replaced by a line of stones
on the sill like prayer books,
that pearl returned to its homely shell
and the desert beyond.

Alma in the Camposantos

Alma walks a path that rises toward silence,
twists like an injured spine
on the body of the low mountain.

Medicine's relics have been at work on her.
Prescriptions and fifty-minute incantations
have performed what magic they can.

Now the pine trees have their turn.
Now the sky makes an attempt.

On a gravel plateau, the Camposantos:
chipped statuary, gravestones among the scrub, the *morada*
a clutch of tinder and wishes for which she has searched.

In the seam between the boards, she sees a tiny Christ,
milagro fastened to the wall, his garish heart
jeweled and thorned in the flat light.

She can see the image of a face fashioned from branches
high on the wall, and searches the modest altar
for fat hammers to pound stakes between ulna
and radius to prevent the body's weight
from tearing palms clean through.

Only abandoned benches and floor and silent altar.
Only sunlight knifing through many cracks.
The meat of thinking suffers.

The rind of pain at her skull is a circlet
of blue static crowning her.
In the Campo behind her, a Virgin in a rinsed jar
hangs her head behind silted glass,
hands clasped in a perfect almond.

Alma turns to the wavering sheets of heat,
drinks from her clear bottle, and tries to pray:

o splinter keeping company with splinter
o air within a rinsed jar

o nail and wrist fastened in loneliness—
something contain me
fasten me, house me

Her pain does not move away
but reaches up and up, meeting
the landscape with gilded pins,
a private crown fastening her to one existence.

Ruth Waiting

Almost day, she walks up the sidewalk,
streetlamp a sulking tulip, the trees a tangle
of lime limbs in the yellowy dawn.
She carries a sullen bouquet of last night's
stockings and her shoes like twin regrets.

Inside, she turns on every lamp
for the cops who are coming
and plans to be dancing then
as she was when her sweetheart
cleared the threshold, a customer
like any lover, pockets thick with money,
his handsomeness swarming like drowsy bees.

That dead man used to whistle
like he knew what was coming,
like the burning seeds of what love did to her
were already tearing through his windpipe.

When they danced, her dress lisped like petals
and he whispered *love is a slipknot of flowers*
and laughed, misstepping.
Then, after so many nights, he said
no more into the receiver
and she was supposed to stay away and didn't.

When the police come, they'll ask her
if her son heard anything, but who doesn't
press their ear to plaster for those dark songs unraveling?
Her boy always loved to sit amidst
the blushing piles of crinoline, the garter belts
and stockings strewn like bodiless women.

What will become of him, she wonders,
swaying as she looks out to the street,
quiet as a new bride, all petal skin, waiting to open.

Surveyor's Camp

Weathered hats cut their faces with shade
and the surveyors squint into the sun,
drink the remains of their coffee,
roll cigarettes and smoke them.
One stares out at the breathing grasses,
tastes the ashen pleasure
of tobacco beneath his tongue,
observes everything at angle
with everything else: coyote loping off straight,
long stalks of grass bending obtuse,
yellow dog asleep perpendicular
to the spoked wagon wheel's acute portions of light.
Even the buffalo shaking the earth at a distance
will bend to the mercy of angle and trajectory,
gods of hinge, pulley, and lathe,
to the powers of alidade, heliostat, octant.
Grease pencils, protractors, compasses wait
in their latched boxes under wagon cover.
The man knows a different nature is throwing
its net over earth and sky.
Tin plates littered in supper scraps and elbows
thick with the labor of progress
crowd the table above its beveled limits.
Finally, campfire under the white moon,
the man can see hard shapes in the sky.
He will help connect them himself,
those rails of some necessary fence.

Billy Dreams He's Dillinger

See how it storms, how it roams inside?
Off the farm and into the streets, infamy
could be brought to the sternum, the eye,
the halo of the self with its powdery gray wonder.
Billy dreamed it: women in bright slips flanking him
with their hidden tongues, their syrupy ennui, and him—
Colt, moonshine, and the stun of reeling half-lit through the day.
Billy knew infamy could be had like ivory,
like gold in the earth, in the teeth of dead men.
If it worked, they would say he walked handsome,
radiant, with landscapes slaked with eternity.
If it worked, a piece of beach from split bone
and no mercy end to end.

Billy climbed the roof at night, lay flat against
the shingles radiating the day's sun, felt
the moon-fastened sky too huge above him.
It stormed, roamed, and he feared nothing on this earth
because he knew so little of it, his ignorance
animating his lithe boy-limbs.
Infamy had, gangsters, gun molls would drive all night
to the wasteland of his Kansas town,
kneel in the dirt above him, break his tombstone
into granite amulets, plant lit Marlboros in the loose grass,
and sprinkle the earth with cheap gin and ash,
drop pocket change among the flowers,
saying *pesetas, pennies, tiny stars.*

After the Strip Club

He leans over the felted lip
and the long chalked bone
slides through the place
he makes for it, little sign for *ok*
as lacquered balls crack and angle
off the long, green borders.
The spheres find the openings
made for them while he swallows gin and bits
of ice, considers trajectories and angles,
waits for the next naked girl
to appear, glazed and spinning.

Soon enough, he staggers out
into the moth-dazzled lights
of almost-morning, searches
the softly lit isolation and considers
what might have become
of his teen daughters, his ex-wife,
his old friend she married.
The baby girl used to eat lemons,
make her mouth an *o*, her eyes shut tight.

Driving home, he passes houses,
rectangular prisms around
sleeping mothers and children
and even fathers. An eye closed
to change two roads to one,
he thinks of geometry and time
and of the bruise-eyed girls always
swaying and shimmering nearby.

The Buick brings him to the right
curb, two wheels on the lawn.
Outside the car, his knees buckle,
then correct, head spinning and sick
as he falls back onto the grass.
The stars overhead are like a scattering
of silver mouths frozen open in surprise.

Still Life with Judas & Lightning

Spindle-armed and sure,
the tree reaches toward him.

Each leaf is designed but cannot be read.

God's marks still shine upon him,
two brilliant thumbprints on his brow bones,
swirls of pollen forgotten.

His tongue lies burning in his mouth.
What can words do now?

The branch offers sanctuary from the world
and its endless choosing,
so he climbs and sits and sees the whole horizon,
its unknowable beauties.
Beauty will not stop him.

As he drops into the air, lightning golden and sharp
slits his body like a blushed
pear and harvests the spirit.

The tree dangles the husk of him.
What is left?

At knee, at hinge of ankle and foot,
at each tarsal of toe, the light leaks,
ignites fiery petals of his finish.

He is seed and leaf. He is rind and stem,
caudex of so many ruined blooms.

Third Person Sacred

Sometimes you know a person's story,
or a piece of it, one sliver of the muscle
examined for its striations and color.
Sometimes you think of your own story
and it is both familiar and not,
and you must question the details,
the slant, the cant of its little roof and shutters,
the home of what you know about yourself,
your people, the city, the schools
and afternoons that made you.

There is someone in your field of vision.
Maybe it is you.
Light spills down on the diorama
and something has brought you here to witness
the holy moment, any moment,
with the gulls overhead like sticks
tossed suddenly skyward and crossing
beneath the biting blueness of the sky.

Prayer

your feet tap
against the edges
of shadow —

learning *agape*
will the change
be worth it?

deciding
is difficult
and the deciding
bruises

comfort has been
such a comfort
you resist
its loss

you examine
whatever happens
searching for something
any flutter
to guide you on

is it proof
: an exhalation of sound
: the visible smudge of soul
  on the glass
: the permeable substance
you know but
can't evidence?

you could shear your hair
old gesture
of grief and reverence
your prickled skull
pleasing eternity
though you are unsure why

in the stream of thinking
you speak to a saint
who is somehow
past the human
and wonder
what to do with that
rune of wonder

a metaphorical hand passes
through you in a dream
to pluck out some
tissue of doubt
without comment
trembling, skinless

each object inside you
unsealed
you receive
an image of yourself
flawed, malformed
but somehow accurate—

the whole project
scares you, the whole
idea of intimacy
with anyone
let alone a saint
let alone someone
who has pushed
past her own
moral stasis
to gain a foothold
let alone yourself

your shadow
—singular and raw—
is unfinished

damage, the "without"
that gives you
your edges
cannot be redeemed
but you seek anyway—

rooted, fluttering, proofless
casting deeply
into the puzzlement
then moving out into the world
with whatever you have

In the Photograph, Lee at Eight

Kneeling in the dirt, he waits
for the photograph to happen.
All around him it is summer.
The scallion in his left hand,
a green question, drops crumbs of soil.
Glasses tilt on his small nose
and he hams it up for the camera.
His future could be anything
as he kneels there. He could
make a choice that would
change the world. Kneeling
in his uncle's field, his lips
are unkissed and silly, his future
never touching him. Later,
his family won't hear from him,
year after year. Where is the seed
of that future in the child?
When this photograph is finished,
he stands and blinks, realizing
there is no one around for miles,
and wheat stands in every direction
like uncounted days.

After Rodin's *Danaïd*

Her arms, spine, flanks twist into the shape
the artist insists upon.
The woman takes the pose, cheek to floor, hip skyward,
face shut in a sleep of some
damnation she's been told to show.
The blankets on the floor beneath her smell of chalk.

When he is finished, she unfurls again into existence,
remade from the person
drowsing in the white load of rock.
That other self she leaves to him,
stuck in stillness
while what is real stands and dresses
and walks outside into the actual air.

Lacy Reading Luke at Twilight

After supper, belly to frayed spread, a story
on translucent pages takes her:
a woman entered a cool corridor, forbidden,
and hurried past the clutch of men to the rabbi.
He wasn't described.
Not bearded, not long-haired, not black-eyed.
Lacy wonders him. He was the man with answers.
There used to be someone who knew what to do
and desperate people travelled far to beg his help.
This one poor woman put her face on his feet,
and was hated and didn't care if she was
because this man might dislodge a great pain.
There was a man walked the earth once,
the story said, and he could fix it.
Did it ail you? He had the tincture,
appeared it from true nothing.
But they hammered that man to boards
and left him all day till dead under the sun.
She knows that part already.
One story said that before the boards,
his living fingers sparked
and he wielded invisible powers
and forgave every day and moment
of that woman's life.
Lacy could see the woman stand up
and meet the eyes of every man,
could see her walk free
except for the burden of healing,
its gashes and sutures and bluish, bruisy halos.
On her back, the day's light spent and scattered.
Lacy wonders *Who gathers the scum off the pond?*
Who helps you up from your knees
and toward that sky full of sparkling judges?

Billy Dreams His Infamous Namesake

This is what fate means: the riverbed bringing up
the body of the one who will prophesy.
Billy, a real kid himself, could not guess the age
of the young man, but it lay in its famous hat,
on water's silvered cot, and waited his approach.
To the hand he went: raw-knuckled, caught as a claw.
The hand had arched streams of urine into gutters,
mended buttoned shirts, scraped the foamy sweat
of horses, clicked bullets into men's soft guts.
A hand once miniature and reaching for cheek, for lip.
Fingers innocent, unremarkable, later closed
around spoons, women's wrists, bottles
of burnished liquor, axe handles, the indigo
ears of dogs wanting to exist.
Its skin had been prepared with unguents:
sweated leather, tobacco leaf, damp onions,
women's inner ointments, lye soap, a fat crush of lilacs.
Its twin is the same: still, finished, historical.
Hip-deep in the river, Billy takes the frozen
hands in his own, and asks

Am I a clutch of chicken bones?
Am I a thatch of fiery sticks soon through?

The water is higher now and the lost man a barge.
It must return now to its portion of dirt
downriver and too far to see
and the bright, dreaming boy
to his bed and unlived future.

A Green Branch & Emily's Worries

It speaks obedience if you let it.

The Klan came through once:
white horsed, white peaked,
breathing death.

A man a few streets away turned on the gas,
murdering his family in their sleep.
He went too. They were found there,
wordless and blue in their familiar beds.

There was a fear, a suffering cut loose.
It roamed long, wouldn't be slaked.

The remedy is worry, Emily thought.
So she learned her worry, its knots,
its stitches. *To leave aside worry
is to await the coming train
while standing on the tracks.*

Things were occurring in the world.
The paper tried to convey a few of them.
She read it daily, parsing, seeking understanding
like just the right thin branch to beat the evil out.

Her worries were those branches.
They'd make her good.

Cell Window

Outside, the sky is only itself
and Michael can walk beneath it,
open his eyes to its vast, unknowable face.
He has waited ten years.
He will wait eighteen hours more
for the gurney with its set of eight
buckled straps, for the bright needles
bearing their three perfect chemicals
and the last mystery.
Someone will capture his words then, he thinks,
and several will watch him twitch into stillness.
He has seen it happen, how the animal
struggles to escape the funnel forcing it to leave the body.
Walking the cement, he looks up to see nature
without the diamonds of the fence, without
the special glass in the tiny window of his cell
which delicately x's the clouds,
the sun itself and the whole horizon.

David at Thirteen, Homeless

The storefronts blaze sunrise.
The river is up. And the birds.
He saw a beaver once at this hour,
lumbering in the brush, moving tiredly
with two kittens a pace away,
had learned the term at school, *kittens*.
He remembers the dust on the windows
of his third-grade classroom waiting
for a word to be written there.
He recalls the worksheets columned
in double digits and the little
dash or cross and the line beneath
and how clear what it was you were expected to do.
The river is always moving.
There are always birds to call out day
when he wakes on the ground,
the tarp radiating cold and the dirt smell like pennies.
A smaller girl stands next to him.
She is new to this life and holds
something close beneath her coat.
Worksheets for her are not so far away,
nor the dust of the windows,
nor a place to walk home.
Her forehead is smudged
and he cannot think of any words.
Their mothers are near and share a cigarette,
letting mercy's small scarf
rise in the air between them.

Zoe Beside Highway 22

Wet and febrile she wakes
and thinks herself
buried and awakened in a blue grave.

Smells of dirt and night air
don't tell her how she has come
to a ditch outside Idanha, but she slips

from the husk of old blanket,
and crawls hand and knee
from the slit of earth.

At the mouth of the ditch,
she finds gravel, distant trees, the highway
with its unending yellow bisection.

Naked and dragging the blanket
like a long caul, she walks the gravel
toward the eyes of cars.

Each vehicle approaches with its beams
and inhuman speed. Mud-smeared, staggering,
she lets the headlights wash her,

illuminate her skin, her very bones, and pass.
Tired, she lies down again beside the road
and looks up at the stars, her witnesses.

They saw what happened and won't say.
The cold wraps her in its black lace.
She does not know how long

until a thin light presses its silver
between her lids and a man covers her in a new
blanket that smells of powdered soap.

Behind him the stars become like blue salvia
crushed down by her body as she was placed
like a memento of what's to come.

Lacy at the Fence Line

Barbed wire keeps the neighbors' cattle in
and her girl-hands fit between the barbs like that.
Holding wire like palm-creases set free,
she feels the prick of barb at rib through her dress.
A mottled calf eyes her from the scrub.
Behind Lacy's left shoulder, her dead mother waits
seven paces back, probably also watching the calf.
Her presence is like the Santa Ana wind,
a fast warmth whirling unseen.
Lacy stands on the sod, outside of life,
holding the sharp wire.
She will not turn to see.
She will listen with perked ear
to the silty, dry words of the dead
as they clamber close
in the blank field, Indian Summer
orange in her eyes
as she watches that calf watching her,
unsure of her, unclear
where the rest of the herd has gone.

Keith Decides to Live Anyway

Days accumulate behind him.
Wind outside moves through leaves
like rumination through memory.
He has done certain things
and they stand at his back
an orchard of ambivalence,
some shameful harvest.
Unstoppable shafts of noon light
bloom shards of coming rain.
Days form an orchard, a corridor of bark and cycles.
Acts have his name on them,
his face, and it is the face he wants hidden
beneath insects in the bark.
Against one length of trunk, his hand
tells stories of what's occurred, carved in
with the tip of a broken stick,
living's little map of the acre:
what he did and what was done to him
and other things that wouldn't fit.
When he walks the orchard, it is twilight.
His shadow attached, still faintly luminous.
Trembling like the foliage, it limps past the pear trees,
keeping him strange company.
Shriveled cores alight with fading rays.
Even as he walks, he is surprised to wonder
Where isn't beauty hidden?

Plum

She has followed the caravan of mystery,
stumbled behind wide-eyed,
eating the crumbs as they fell.
She has watched someone making miracles—
corpse, water cask, maps of lesions, empty net—
and suddenly her little soul appears,
housed in her body
like the pit of a plum:
gnarled, intricate, a perfect whorl
within the orange damp.
Or like the glistening gospel of viscera
within the fish slit and readied for supper.
Something waiting for a new use, ready to be seen.
She waits to understand.
But she does not.

So she returns home.
Lavender still brushes the crooked steps.
The table is still the same silent square.
Beyond the yard: an unending field
and fruit ready for gleaning.
Plums have fallen into hot grass
unconsumed, an extravagance
of sweetness laid to waste.

Each morning she takes a single plum,
bites juice and fruit to pit,
then blesses that remnant in her palm:
a tiny labyrinth of wild bone,
that small permanence.

Notes

"Hana Is *Flower"*
after Hitoshi Igarashi, translator of Salman Rushdie's *The Satanic Verses*
into Japanese, stabbed to death in 1991

"The Artists' Angels"
Petrus Christus, *The Nativity* (c.1445)
Hans Memling, *Madonna and Child with Angels* (c.1480)
Domenico Veneziano, *St. Francis Receiving the Stigmata* (c.1445/1450)
Jan van Eyck, *The Annunciation* (c.1425/1430)
Gian Lorenzo Bernini, *Ecstasy of St. Teresa* (1647–1652)
Francesco del Cossa, *St. Lucy* (1473)

"Enshrined Outlaw as Seven Relics"
after Jesse James, American bank and train robber; Zee was his wife's name

"Alma in the Camposantos"
The *morada* is a chapel used by Penitentes, lay Catholics, primarily found
in New Mexico, who practice penitential worship.

"Ruth Waiting"
after Ruth Ellis, the last woman executed in England

"Surveyor's Camp"
after an 1842 photograph of a camp in the Dakotas

"Billy Dreams His Infamous Namesake"
after William H. Bonney, or William H. McCarty, Jr., known as "Billy the
Kid"

Acknowledgments

Thanks to the editors of the publications of the following journals in which these poems first appeared, often in an altered version:
Dogwood: A Journal of Poetry and Prose, "Runaway Slave Resting in the Brush at Dawn"; *Paddlefish*, "Hagar & the Blue Jay at the Buena Vista Apartments"; *Piedmont Literary Review*, "Bonnie in the Woods"; *The Brooklyn Review*, "Young Widow in the Field"; *Willow Review*, "In the Photograph, Lee at Eight"; *ZYZZYVA*, "John Eight"; *Berkeley Poetry Review*, "Still Life with Judas & Lightning"; *Red Cedar Review*, "Enshrined Outlaw as Seven Relics"; *Southern Poetry Review*, "When Lazarus Comes Back"; *Portland Review*, "The Rinsing Sink"; *Beloit Poetry Journal*, "Trapeze in Autumn"; *The Iowa Review*, "Prayer."

Thank you as well to the editors of Airlie Press for their generosity of spirit and time, to Monica and Deanne for so many years, to Klaus for the cover image and his kindness, and to the Feminati for being the seed of the tree.

About the Publisher

Airlie Press is run by writers. A nonprofit publishing
collective, the press is dedicated to producing beautiful
and compelling books of poetry. Its mission is to offer
writers working in its particular habitat a local, shared-work
publishing alternative. Airlie Press is supported by book
sales, subscription orders, and donations. All funds return
to the press for the creation of new books of poetry.

Other Titles from Airlie Press

Colophon

Titles and text are set in Warnock Light,
part of a font family designed in 2000
by Robert Slimbach, a recipient of the
Charles Peignot Award for excellence in type design.